THE LITTLE BOOK OF GRATITUDE

LEARN HOW TO PRACTICE GRATITUDE AND USE IT TO CHANGE YOUR LIFE

JENNIFER SPARKS

STOKE PUBLISHING

The Little Book of Gratitude

YOU NEED A BEAUTIFUL JOURNAL TO WRITE IN, SO MAKE SURE YOU HAVE ONE ON HAND.
Enjoy the journey!

Disclaimer: I am not a doctor, nutritionist, magician or dietician. I am sharing what has worked personally for me, and while I hope that you will find some of the information and ideas helpful, implementing it into your own life is done so at your own discretion.

Paperback ISBN: 978-1-988675-36-7
Ebook ISBN: 978-1-988675-51-0

BULK ORDERS/REDUCED PRICING
www.jennifersparks.ca

DEDICATION

To you.

Because you have taken a step towards crafting a life of abundance and bliss. May your journey towards a solid practice of gratitude be rewarding & joyful.

You are surrounded by blessings, may you be able to see and appreciate them in full colour.

In times of hardship, lean into gratitude to find your way to a better place.

CONTENTS

WORDS OF GRATITUDE

I am grateful for understanding that I am exactly where I am supposed to be, and all that happens to me (for me) teaches me the lessons I need to learn, grow and expand. Indeed, some of these lessons are painful, but I am thankful I have learned to understand that even in pain, there is beauty. Without this understanding, the darker days would have seemed unbearable. Gratitude has been my lifeline on more days than I can count. I hope it can serve you in the same way.

As always, I feel compelled to acknowledge my friends and family for their support. There have been many days of deep challenge and my friends and family have had my back, been my breath and kept me sane.

For all the strong entrepreneurial women in my circle, who believe that women can join forces for the greater good, you make this world a better place. Thank you for your inspiration and all you do to share my work with others.

INTRODUCTION

This journal has been created to introduce, explore and give structure to the practice of gratitude. While the practice of gratitude is quite simple, sometimes a loving nudge can help you find your own sweet spot to make the practice belong to you. You have to own it, believe in it and experience the magic if you are to truly integrate a gratitude mindset into your life.

Gratitude is something that may begin as a clumsy attempt to "count your blessings," but it can have a way of grabbing hold of you and working its way deep into your heart and mind. And then a shift in focus, energy and joy follows. Gratitude changes lives. I know this because it has transformed my own life and many of my coaching clients' lives as well. Research has shown that there is a positive link between gratitude journaling and overall wellbeing (Emmons & McCullough 2003). For those of us who have spent time buried in the pages of our journals, we understand this magic.

However, when the focus of the journal becomes gratitude, the impact is further enhanced.

This summer, in a cabin tucked in the trees in northern Saskatchewan, my mother and I sat talking about how the practice of gratitude has changed our lives. I asked her if she consciously practiced gratitude before I wrote about it in my books, and she said no, but went on to say that she walks out of the house every day now and simply says thank you for each new day. She pays attention to the small details. She recognizes that there is plenty to celebrate even on the bad days. It is so easy to take all our blessings for granted. We have to train ourselves to filter our environments in a particular way and when we do, a profound shift can occur.

I could never have made it through my daughter's initial diagnosis of epilepsy and subsequent seizure management without learning to use gratitude to control my stress and anxiety. I was trying to control things I could never expect to realistically control. Much like trying to hold the wind in an open hand, the tighter I held on and tried to control what I had no control over, the more out of control I spun. As I like to say, *sometimes you need to let go to get a better grip.*

The simple practice of gratitude can increase your happiness, optimism, compassion and immune system. It can also help you deal with anxiety, depression and loneliness (Emmons & McCullough 2003). Gratitude can be used in partnership with other strategies and medical interventions to help depression. Research has shown that gratitude alone can increase your happiness by as much as 25 percent (Emmons, 2007). And, as Sonja Lyubomirsky has shared in her research about happiness, up to 40 percent of an individual's happiness is in his or her ability to change, with gratitude playing a large role in her findings.

Some days when I look around, I wonder why it appears to be socially acceptable to be unhappy, overworked and overwhelmed rather than excited and thankful for the simple things that bring us joy. Have we moved so far off our centre that we are completely caught up in the hustle and bustle of chasing things? Have we forgotten how to savour a moment and to be appreciative of all the gifts that surround us? Did we ever actually know how to *consciously* do this or is this a skill we need to learn to consciously apply into our lives?

Of all the strategies I have incorporated into my life, the practice of gratitude has been the most powerful. Yet, it seemed almost trivial. It has shifted my focus more times than I can count, reduced my stress and made me love my life even when I didn't love everything that was going on in my life (or when circumstances were less than ideal.) It has allowed me to put one foot in front of the other and have hope that I would be okay, even when circumstances should have totally overwhelmed me.

Gratitude has given me superhuman coping skills, and I truly believe gratitude can help many people become more fulfilled and less stressed. That is why this journal has been created in the manner that it has.

To save time and space here, I won't go into all the details of my own journey, but if you wish to learn more about it or to learn about the tools and strategies I used to change my life, I have shared it all in my best-selling books *WTF to OMG: The Frazzled Female's Guide to Creating a Life You Love* and *Happy on Purpose*. Both of these books are action guides should you be looking for guidance on how to begin changing your life and moving towards the life you have dreamed of living.

But for now, we focus on GRATITUDE!

TAKING COURAGEOUS ACTION

*If I had waited for things to be perfect before I made a move, I would never have done anything remarkable. The greatest gift I have ever given myself is accepting myself for the absolutely imperfect human that I am. Scars, flaws and mistakes galore are what make me uniquely me. And you uniquely you. Understanding that perfection is a myth and taking courageous action despite my fears, has allowed me to accomplish dreams and participate in my life more fully. Life has taught me that in all moments, there is something worth appreciating and being grateful for, but I had to teach myself to see these things. I struggled for a long time. Learning to trust in the power of gratitude has changed my life. ~*Jennifer Sparks

When I had found myself in a place of absolute despair, I knew something had to change. I was afraid. Afraid of failure, mistakes, more pain and hard choices. Almost accidentally, I began to count my blessings as a way to stay afloat. I had no idea at the time what this courageous action would ignite within me. I didn't know if I could even muster up a list of things I was grateful for, but I tried it anyway.

My initial blessings seemed almost trivial, because both my life and mental state were in absolute chaos. I started by acknowledging that I was grateful for simply breathing each day. Then I began to notice other things. I relished a warm, creamy coffee. I noted when the hot sun caught my face through the window on a cold winter's morning, and I sat in stillness and savoured that moment consciously. I took notice when I heard my children laughing, and realized how it brought me joy because that carefree, untethered laughter had somehow slowly vanished in recent months. Gradually, I began to sense a shift in the way I perceived the world. Nothing had changed, yet everything had. As I looked for three simple things to write down each evening, I began to turn my back on the negativity in my life, and sought out the beautiful things instead, even if they were mere moments in a very long, overwhelming day. Often simple and free and right beneath my nose, my life bloomed with the practice of gratitude and yours can too.

As we move through this little book on gratitude, you will be given assignments and tasks to explore. Each assignment is designed to expose you to the magic of gratitude in very different ways. Each assignment approaches the practice from a different angle and headspace. Each will give you a different experience or lesson. After you have practiced gratitude in various ways, you will be better equipped to make some choices about how you wish to continue your gratitude transformation.

Each one of us may select a different approach to continuing our practice and that is really the point: you must own your practice, feel the magic in it, feel that the practice is lifting you up and keeping your mindset healthy. I can't tell you what is right for you, but as you work your way through this journal, you will discover and create your own methods. **This journal is your personal experiment.**

For the first week, your assignment is simple. All you need to do is write down three things you are grateful for each evening. They can be little things. They can seem trite and superficial. The objective here is to make you hyper-aware of these smaller things so you begin to take notice of all the things that you are grateful for with increasing ease. This process will begin to remove the blinders we all wear when we move through life disconnected from our blessings.

Grab your journal and list the days and capture on paper - three things each day you are grateful to have in your life for seven consecutive days.

When you are all done, it is time to reflect.

Reflections

Writing the first things that come to mind, how does it feel to have successfully focused on your blessings for the past seven days?

Did it change the way you see your environment?

Did you feel your focus shifting as the week progressed?

Explain. Get busy in your journal and climb deep inside your heart.

2

DIGGING DEEPER

"IN THE DEPTHS OF DISAPPOINTMENT WHAT IS REALLY MISSING IS ... GRATITUDE." ~ BRENDON BURCHARD, AUTHOR

There are many ways to practice gratitude, and how you decide to integrate the practice into your life and routine is your choice. The initial chapters of this book are designed to give you experience with several approaches so you can best decide how to continue on your own. The truth is, you will not continue practicing gratitude if you have no experience with the benefit of trying, so please give yourself a fair chance to see this magic at work.

Last week, you simply took stock of the blessings all around you. The objective of this was to turn ON your gratitude radar. This week, we will dig deeper by selecting one thing you are grateful for and then listing *five reasons why* you are grateful for the item you selected. This does something different to you, so be open and have fun. Feel your heart reach towards all the goodness that surrounds you. Breath deep and dig deeper.

Grab your journal and use this framework each day for a week.

Day 1

I am grateful for _____ and here are the five reasons why:

1.

2.

3.

4.

5.

WHEN YOU HAVE COMPLETED this task, please take the time to continue in your journal to capture your reflections.

Reflections

Writing the first things that come to mind, how does it feel to have held yourself accountable for understanding why you are grateful for the items you listed?

Did digging deeper help you feel a more profound sense of gratitude? Explain.

What connections did you make between the things you are grateful for and the joy in your life? Explain.

THROWING THE GRATITUDE NET WIDE

"LIFE IS AMAZING. AND THEN IT'S AWFUL. AND
THEN IT'S AMAZING AGAIN. AND IN BETWEEN THE
AMAZING AND THE AWFUL IT'S ORDINARY AND
MUNDANE AND ROUTINE. BREATHE IN THE
AMAZING, HOLD ON THROUGH THE AWFUL, AND
RELAX AND EXHALE DURING THE ORDINARY.
THAT'S JUST LIVING A HEARTBREAKING, SOUL-
HEALING, AMAZING, AWFUL, ORDINARY LIFE. AND
IT'S BREATHTAKINGLY BEAUTIFUL." ~L.R. KNOST

Going **deep** into the reasons behind your gratitude is a powerful practice in opening your heart and your mind. It begins to shift your perceptions about particular people, events or things in your worldview. However, going **wide** teaches you to see it everywhere, especially in places where you do not even think it is possible to see it.

Going wide teaches you to sift through the muck of everyday, overwhelming life so you can learn to hand-pick these little gems that are surrounding you. Zen Master and Spiritual Leader Thich Nhat Hanh explains that "we need the mud to make the lotus flower." If we are to become fully developed people, our hard times contribute just as much to that development as the good times, perhaps even more so! Experiencing pain and sorrow allows us to fully appreciate happiness and joy!

So how do we go wide? We list as many things as we can that we are grateful for in our current lives! It all counts: from the crisp apple we can enjoy in the sunshine, to the creamy coffee we sip leisurely with a friend, to the sweet kisses our children smear across our faces, to the deep breath we can take when we need to step back from this crazy, beautiful, fast-paced world.

Grab your journal and let's do this!

Let's keep this simple and start with listing fifty things. You have a week to complete this list. Look every-where. When you find yourself stressed and anxious, look even more then. When you feel tired and over-whelmed, stop and take in your environment. Slowly scan your heart, mind and memory for the slivers of joy … they are there but you need to learn to see them, perhaps for the very first time.

Enjoy this process and please feel free to share your list on social media #littlebookofgratitude. I love learning about new ways to see the world and there is nothing like a list of 50 things someone is grateful for to really shift your take on life.

Reflections

Has anything shifted about how you feel about your life?

THE LITTLE BOOK OF GRATITUDE

Do you see things to be grateful for where you didn't expect to see them? Explain.

"Rejoicing in ordinary things is not sentimental or trite. It actually takes guts. Each time we drop our complaints and allow everyday good fortune to inspire us, we enter the warrior's world. We can do this even at the most difficult moments. Everything we see, hear, taste and smell has the power to strengthen and uplift us." ~ Pema Chödrön

---

4

PUT IT IN WRITING

"THE STRUGGLE ENDS WHEN GRATITUDE BEGINS."
~NEALE DONALD WALSH

Thus far in your journey, your focus may have been on things, events or savoured solo moments, but you are also surrounded by people who have made a positive difference in your life. Now is the time to list some of the people who have really impacted you in a positive way. Then, select one (or if you are really keen, all of them) and put in writing what their presence in your life has meant to you.

The rough draft can go below, and then you can write out a good copy for passing along to your special person. While we may often think grateful thoughts and bounce them around in our own minds, how often do we share them? Do we release the energy that gratitude creates so others can benefit as well?

Imagine the impact of receiving a letter of gratitude from someone you have connected with and supported in your own life. There is tremendous power in sharing and it is an often forgotten part of the gratitude practice. Imagine that each time you share with someone how they have impacted your life, you get to feel the gratitude once again, and they, in turn, get to feel appreciated and cherished. This challenge allows you to magnify your gratitude and give something back to those who have helped you out!

The Ten People I Am Grateful To Have In My Life

1.

2.

3.

4.

5.

6.

7.

8.

. . .

9.

10.

THE ASSIGNMENT

Taking one name from the list above (or several depending on your wishes) craft a letter thanking the person for the positive role he/she has played in your life and personal development. Do not fret over the length of your note, but focus on content. Be specific. Understand that as you write, the impact of your gratitude will have an effect on him/her when he/she receives it. Make sure to share how his/her presence in your life in this capacity has impacted you as a person.

You have all week to write this letter and pop it in the mail. Understand that this is incredibly powerful and you are releasing an energy into the atmosphere that will forever change the recipient in some way as well.

Really, you are changing the world.

A SHIFTING PERSPECTIVE

"THE MORE YOU USE IT, THE STRONGER IT
GROWS, AND THE MORE POWER YOU HAVE TO
USE IT ON YOUR BEHALF. IF YOU DO NOT
PRACTICE GRATEFULNESS, ITS BENEFACTION WILL
GO UNNOTICED, AND YOUR CAPACITY TO DRAW
ON ITS GIFTS DIMINISHED. TO BE GRATEFUL IS TO
FIND BLESSINGS IN EVERYTHING. THIS IS THE
MOST POWERFUL ATTITUDE TO ADOPT, FOR
THERE ARE BLESSINGS IN EVERYTHING." ~ALAN
COHEN

Life sucks sometimes. Gratitude can save you from these moments of despair because it shifts your focus from what is NOT going right to what IS going right. Things will not always be as you want them to be. Sometimes life will not go your way for a very long period of time and you may struggle to keep believing that things will eventually be okay again. You may struggle knowing that things will be forever different on the other side of a challenging stage of life.

When things hit the skids and life throws you the ever famous curve ball, hold tight to the practice of gratitude and use it to put things into perspective. Gratitude can help you see the possible opportunities for growth and advancement within your times of struggle.

Life can be very hard, and it can seem like everything is going wrong, but remember that there is always someone out there who would do anything to just be in your shoes. Things could always be worse regardless of your situation, so choose to focus on the good and lean on that. When you feel like a major load of lemons just got dumped on your door step, take a big step backwards and an even bigger breath and answer the following questions:

- What is the lesson in this event that I can take with me moving forward to further develop as a person? (These may be very hard lessons. I am sorry for that.)
- How can I benefit from this experience?
- Can I find three things within this situation that I can be grateful for?
- Can I list a few things that are good about this event or goodness that came about as a result of this event?
- How could things be worse?

Several of my clients have gone through difficult divorces and it is very hard to find a list of positives when you are knee deep in the muck of it all. But I always encourage them to humor me and look for a few perks anyways. If there are children as a result of the marriage, they are often a blessing that is easy to identify. However, if single parenting is overwhelming them, then it may be hard to see it that way at first.

As time moves on, and as the process of divorce unfolds, new experiences begin to take place and these clients can find themselves easily being grateful for the opportunity to try something new. I often hear, "If I was still married I never would have had the chance to experience this because he/she hated this kind of stuff."

It is also common for people who have been in loveless marriages to be devastated when it ends simply because they do not know what is next, but with some guidance they can learn to see that uncertainty can be exciting. They don't realize it at the time, but they are often just fearful of the loss of routine and structure and they do not see the opportunities they have before them to totally redesign their lifestyle without input from a significant other. This allows them to truly follow their own north star at a later stage in their life when their interests and desires are more refined. What might look like "complete destruction" can actually be the ground work for something truly magnificent.

As life begins anew, people often find the dating process a weary, hopeless task until one day they meet THE person that changes everything and gives them an entirely new perspective on relationships. In this moment, it is easy to find gratitude for the demise of a marriage, because without that breakdown, they would never have learned the lessons they needed to learn to be in this moment in time, as the person they are now, to meet this new person and to be the individual the new person is strongly attracted to. As we move forward, we may find that the hardest days of our lives become the things we learn to be most grateful for!

The Assignment

Think back to a time when you felt overwhelmed and hopeless. Record your version of the event. Return to the five questions posed earlier in this chapter and work through them with this specific event in mind. What have you learned and how does this approach shift your perspective of the event you had identified? And as always, reflect on how this activity made you feel.

"For a seed to achieve its greatest expression, it must come completely undone. The shell cracks, its insides come out and everything changes. To someone who doesn't understand growth, it would look like complete destruction."

~Cynthia Occelli

6

LET'S GET PERSONAL

"GRATITUDE IS A MAGNETIC ENERGY THAT DRAWS
PEOPLE TO US." ~ ANNE LAMOTT

Aside from the letters you mailed earlier, have you **personally expressed your gratitude** to someone who has made an impact in your life? Even if the answer is yes, now is the time. Several years ago, I met a beautiful woman on Facebook who was struggling to leave a marriage and create happiness for herself and young family. I connected with her because I recognized my former self in her. Three or four years have passed and I have watched with great pleasure to see her life unfold beautifully. Tonight, out of the blue, she messaged me and said, *"I just wanted to reach out and tell you that without meeting you, I adore you. I'm so grateful for the love you showed me in the absolute darkest moments of my life."*

WOW. What do I say to that?

I have a bond with this women and I have never met her. I saw her pain, reached out and shared my own stories and strategies with her in attempt to try to ease her pain. Years passed and she has not forgotten our exchanges. I had not forgotten her either, and I was always thrilled to see life working out for her and her family. The fact that she messaged me to let me know I made a difference made me emotional and even more grateful. **It also reminded me that we never know how deep one act of kindness can reach.** Now imagine how this would have gone down if we had met for lunch face to face! That is what this week's assignment is all about: personal connection, eye contact, a heartfelt hug and perhaps even tears of joy.

Who do you have to thank? What exactly did they do that made an impact in your life? Now is the time to reach out and let them know and in doing so, you will be impacting them in a positive way, too. This is about celebrating connection!

Three People I Am Grateful To Have In My Life

1.

2.

3.

Now set up appointments to meet these people in person to personally express your gratitude to them. Book a coffee date or dinner and take your time to make sure they understand how powerful of a force their kindness was in your life. Observe them as you share your gratitude and savour the emotional connection.

Write about how you feel as you set up these appointments and what happens. You may feel some anxiety but, again, you are about the change the world and a human with your gratitude.

Reflections

Record what took place in your face-to-face gratitude meeting.

How did you feel?

How did the other person/people feel and did they share their emotions with you?

Any ripples of joy result from your inspired action?

7

GRATITUDE WALKS

"WALK AS IF YOU ARE KISSING THE EARTH WITH
YOUR FEET." THICH NHAT HANH

One day when my daughter was riding her horse at the barn, I went for a walk. I was feeling under the weather and physically weak. I was frustrated by this but I knew I needed a good dose of nature and fresh air. I wanted to run but I knew I didn't have it in me to manifest that level of energy. So instead, I walked.

I started off on my walk trying to listen to some podcasts on my iPod but I soon felt agitated from the intrusion into my thoughts so I unplugged and took a slow, deep breath. As I walked, I took notice of the little things. For the first time ever I noticed that prickly, undesired thistles bloomed a vibrant purple. Imagine that! Even thistles, like prickly people, can be beautiful.

I took note of other road side flowers that were beautiful, small and virtually unnoticed in their beauty as I seldom walked this road, but instead drove it at a speed that blurred its glorious details into boring roadside.

The beauty had been there all along, I had just never taken the time to notice.

I memorized the old bird boxes on the farm fences, weathered and worn but looking like a vintage post-cards. I noticed the sounds of the birds and stopped to observe a nest of hawks flying high above, screeching and hunting. I saw a small fox in the field watch me and then bounce through the grass until I could no longer see him. I paid attention to the sun on my face in one direction and its warming touch on my back in the other direction. I felt the gentle breeze across my face and in my hair. This walk did more for my aching, sore, fatigued body and mind than anything else had done that week. I walked myself into an uplifting, ener-gized mindset.

Sometimes we just need to slow down enough to drink in the goodness that surrounds us. The blue sky, wispy white clouds, the fresh air, and the crunch of rocks under foot. Often it is too easy to dismiss these small delights because they are always there and your mind ignores them. A gratitude walk can leave you feeling refreshed and energized, and it doesn't cost a thing.

In all honesty, when I think of the healing and stress-releasing power of a daily walk, and I pair that activity with the practice of gratitude, I shouldn't be surprised with the calming sense of wellbeing that follows. I am an advocate of daily activity of some kind, and a walk is a great starting point for most. Furthermore, because walking is not strenuous, you can really focus your mind on paying attention to the things around you rather than, let's say, the pain that you experience when running hill repeats.

Now it is your turn. Take a walk. Leave the technology behind unless you feel inclined to take pictures of the beautiful things you notice.

Pay attention to the sounds, smells and sensations. When you look at things, raise your awareness level and truly see them. Stop. Investigate. Touch. Feel. Inhale. Drink in the goodness that surrounds you.

Watch a sunset in silence or a sunrise with a warm coffee in hand as you make your way down a quiet road... walk in gratitude and then return home and record the experience below.

Reflections

Record what took place on your gratitude walk. Capture the smallest details and use all your senses to recall your walk.

Update: I had a client read this section and she shared with me that she did a gratitude clean. She went on to explain, she lives modestly but while cleaning and really taking note of all the things she had around her that she loved and enjoyed, she felt grateful and supported in the end. So take this activity and put your own twist on it!

8

CREATING YOUR GRATITUDE PRACTICE

"GRATITUDE IS NOT ONLY THE GREATEST OF
VIRTUES, BUT THE PARENT OF ALL OTHERS." ~
MARCUS TULLIUS CICERO

The first weeks of this journal were designed to get you thinking outside of the box. The assignments were designed to stretch your thoughts and actions, to encourage reflection and to create a pathway for you to experience gratitude in varied ways. As you well understand, the various approaches of expressing gratitude can yield different results and different emotional responses.

From here on out, use your personal journal to capture your evolving and personal gratitude journey. Capture your gratitude in the manner that best suits who you are as a person and whom you are transforming to be.

Should you become stuck or disenchanted, return to the previous week's work and read your reflections. Embrace the magic you experienced doing some of the earlier tasks. Remind yourself this is a journey, not a destination. If you still feel the need to further explore

9

gratitude, I am leaving you with a small list of other things to try.

Use one of these questions as a spring board for a gratitude journal entry.

- What inspired you today?
- Who inspired you today?
- What negative thought came to mind today and how can you change it into a positive one?
- Describe a negative event and the positive lessons you took from it.
- What made you smile today?
- What made you laugh today?
- What was the most delightful sound you heard today?
- What act of love did you witness today?
- What act of kindness did you witness today?
- What was the best thing that happened this week?
- What was the most luxurious thing you touched today?

◆ **Listomania:** Make a list of the things you are grateful for but divide the list into categories such as: health, finances, career, relationships, spirituality/religion, leisure/recreation, assets, experiences, personal qualities, things that are free and so forth. How big can you make this list?

◆ **Gratitude Meal:** Option 1 - At family meal time go around the table and ask everyone to talk about what the best part of their day was and to explain it in detail so others can share in the joy. (For Special Family Meals & Extended Families.)

♦ **Gratitude Meal:** Option 2 - Place an index card and pencil at each setting. Each person writes the person's name sitting to their left on the card. Then, they write something positive about that person on the card. Once done, they pass the card to their right. Each index card will make it all the way around the table and then back to the person who everyone has praised. What a feel good takeaway from a family gathering!

♦ **Gratitude Jar:** Pick any day to begin this practice. Purchase a pretty coloured glass jar or decorate one with your children or partner. Any time you or a family member has a thought of gratitude, write it on a slip of paper, sign your name, fold it, and drop it in the Gratitude Jar. Every three to six months, have a gratitude celebration and open the jar and read aloud all of the thoughts. This allows you a glimpse into the grateful thoughts of the others with whom you live. We all walk around lost in our own thoughts and this practice allows people to experience a glimpse into the thoughts of others. In addition, you may be way more appreciated than others let you know!

Please remember that gratitude does not have to be practiced on a daily basis as our brains have a way of adjusting to the daily ritual. Lyubomirsky et al. (2005) discovered that those who practiced gratitude once per week were happier than those who practiced three times a week. This suggests that there is some loss in the benefit due to familiarization. Much like an exercise program, our bodies and brains become accustomed to doing something on a regular basis and it is good to shake it up and be a little unpredictable.

Have some fun. Be creative. Invent new activities. Reach out and connect with others. Think gratefully and then share your grateful thoughts with the world through your actions. Bring them to life.

See the world in a new way and experience the magic of a gratitude transformation.

"All we have is all we need. All we need is the awareness of how blessed we really are." ~ Sarah Ban Breathnach

---

9

YOUR JOURNEY FORWARD

"JUST AN OBSERVATION: IT IS IMPOSSIBLE TO BE
BOTH GRATEFUL AND DEPRESSED. THOSE WITH A
GRATEFUL MINDSET TEND TO SEE THE MESSAGE
IN THE MESS. AND EVEN THOUGH LIFE MAY
KNOCK THEM DOWN, THE GRATEFUL FIND
REASONS, IF EVEN SMALL ONES, TO GET UP." ~
STEVE MARABOLI

Now it is your turn to take what you have experienced and transfer it into your personalized gratitude practice. It is up to you alone to see the message in your mess and it is up to you to stay consciously aware that you are in control of what thoughts you choose to focus on as you move through each moment of your day.

You can do no wrong as you take the time each week to slow down and examine your life as it unfolds. **What stories are you telling yourself now that will gently morph into new stories that hold blessings and joy as their core message and how will this new perspective seep effortlessly into all facets of your life as you are transformed from gratitude alone?**

Enjoy the journey and embrace all that makes you smile and takes your breath away!

ABOUT THE AUTHOR
JENNIFER SPARKS

Jennifer Sparks is a life strategist, reiki master, speaker, and author. Her journey to health and wellness has been a long one and over the last ten years she has been focused on learning what helps people implement and sustain healthy lifestyle changes.

She is the bestselling author of *WTF to OMG: The Frazzled Female's Guide to Creating a Life You Love* and *Happy On Purpose: What Happy People Do Differently.* She has also created *The LIFEMAP Infinity Planner* in an effort to help people manage their day to day habits while moving towards their ideal life! She speaks, hosts retreats and coaches some truly brave souls!

Jennifer lives in Saskatoon, Saskatchewan, but considers the world her playground.

Connect with Her: www.jennifersparks.ca

WTF to OMG: The Frazzled Female's Guide to Creating a Life You Love is designed to get you personally connected to understanding WHY mindsets can make or break your spirit and how to use them to overhaul your life and your life's purpose. Liberally sprinkled with hilarious and moving real-life stories that demonstrate the power of a mindset shift, WTF to OMG is the perfect guide for getting unstuck, discovering your life purpose, and creating a life you love. WTF to OMG offers strategies you can apply quickly to become fully aware of what you need to do to create your dream life. Jennifer's approach is gentle but her message is clear: "Your job is to dream big, accept responsibility, and get moving!"

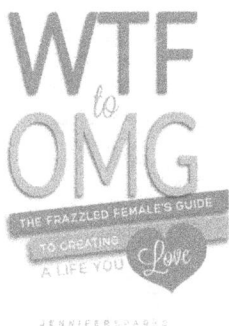

WTF
to
OMG

THE FRAZZLED FEMALE'S GUIDE
TO CREATING
A LIFE YOU *Love*

JENNIFER SPARKS

Happy on Purpose: What Happy People Do Differently explores what happy people do differently and how these differences create a happy life, often despite less than desirable circumstances. Through engaging and honest stories, Jennifer demonstrates that happiness is something that we can choose to create if we are prepared to step out of our comfort zones, examine our social conditioning, and explore our desires more fully. True to her down-to-earth style, Jennifer entices you to connect to the transparent and vulnerable examples she shares about her own struggle to create sustainable happiness. By the time you flip the final page, you will undoubtedly know that you are not alone and that happiness is possible regardless of where you currently are in your own journey. It is up to all of us to be *Happy on Purpose.*

HAPPY
ON PURPOSE

JENNIFER SHARPE
Bestselling author of WTF to OMG